Calico Zebra

by

Julie Bray

DORRANCE PUBLISHING CO
EST. 1920
PITTSBURGH, PENNSYLVANIA 15238

Dorrance Publishing Co
585 Alpha Drive
Suite 103
Pittsburgh, PA 15238
Visit our website at www.dorrancebookstore.com

ISBN: 979-8-88729-353-0
eISBN: 979-8-88729-853-5

Calico Zebra

Zack the Zebra was not a happy zebra. He wanted to be different. He was tired of wearing stripes like everyone else. He decided he wanted spots.

Zack didn't know how to get spots. He decided that he would ask his friends. He found his friend, Gina the Giraffe. He asked Gina how she got her spots. Gina thought about it and said, "Try using juice because it leaves spots on the rug."

Zack had Gina squirt him with orange and grape juice. This did not work. Zack decided to ask someone else. He found his friend, Pete the Python. He asked Pete how he got his spots. Pete thought about it and said, "Try using my old skin because it has spots."

Zack squeezed into Pete's old skin. This did not work. Zack decided to ask someone else. He found his friend, Dawn the Dalmatian. He asked Dawn how she got her spots. Dawn thought about it and said, "Try spraying off the stripes with the firehose."

Zack had Dawn spray him with the firehose. This did not work. Zack decided to ask someone else. He found his friend, Callie the Calico Cat. He asked Callie how she got her spots. Callie thought about it and said, "Try licking off the stripes."

Zack tried licking off the stripes. This did not work. Zack decided to ask someone else. He found Oliver, the wise old owl. He asked Oliver why none of his ideas worked. Oliver thought about it and said, "Your ideas did not work because even though you changed your outside you are still a zebra on the inside." Zack began to cry.

Oliver told Zack, "Even though you look like other zebras, you are still special and shouldn't need to change how you look to stand out. You just need to be true to yourself and your uniqueness will shine through."

Zack looked at himself and thought how funny he looked with spots of all sorts. He listened to Oliver the Owl and decided he did like his stripes, but he could just wear a sweater sometimes.